How To Be Lucky

How To Be Lucky

by Jill Breckenridge

BLUESTEM PRESS
Emporia State University

Acknowledgments

Some of the poems in this volume were initially published in periodicals as follows:

Great River Review: "Fallout," "Sanctuary," "How To Be Lucky," "One More For The Road," "Bottled," "Drawing Of My Family: Age 6," "Christmas Eve, The Morning After," "My Mother's Hands," "Salesman Of The Year."

Kansas Quarterly: "Love Letter From Acapulco."

Looking For Home: Women Writing About Exile (Milkweed Editions): "Bottled," "Unlocking The Door."

Poetry Now: "Cashmere Disciple."

Saturday's Women (Saturday Press): "Transmutations."

Warm Journal: "Helen Hart's Summer Watercolor Class."

Woman Poet, The Midwest: "Attitudes of Thanksgiving."

Library of Congress Cataloging-in-Publication Data

Breckenridge, Jill.
    How to be lucky / by Jill Breckenridge.
        p.   cm.
    ISBN 1-878325-03-5 : $16.95. — ISBN 1-878325-02-7 (pbk.)
        : $8.00
    1. Poetry.   I. Title.
PS3552.R362H6 1990   90-47695
811'.54—dc20   CIP

Bluestem Press books are published by the English Department, Emporia State University, Emporia, Kansas 66801, and distributed by Small Press Distribution, 1814 San Pablo Ave., Berkeley, CA 94702.

The Author Wishes To Thank:

— two fine poets and teachers, Ellen Bryant Voigt and Lisel Mueller;

— my five children;

— my brother, Chad Breckenridge, and his wife, Sally Brown Breckenridge;

— friends, Phebe Hanson, Deborah Keenan, Roseann Lloyd, Jim Moore, David Mura, and the other members of my writing group;

— Adult Children of Alcoholic Parents groups and other 12-step groups;

— those organizations and locations that helped give birth to this book: The Ragdale Foundation in Lake Forest, Illinois, for granting me time and space; The Loft: A Center for Writers, for encouraging readings of the work and crucial cross-pollinization; the North Shore of Lake Superior, where I write and regenerate; and the West, where my deepest symbols formed.

And, finally, my gratitude to my parents, Josephine St. Clair and Charles Corder Breckenridge.

Contents

For John Fenn

I.

The Home Front

Drawing Of My Family: Age 6

One cloud above a white house,
one mother, a little girl,
a father sitting in his blue car,
as the cloud rains under itself.

In my childhood drawing, a sidewalk
reaches from the front door to a road
where the car drives away.

Black smoke curls out of the chimney,
black V birds flap away from the tree,

the blue sky doesn't leave, nor the mother
in her red coat with twelve buttons,
all of them fastened, even the one

under her round head, turned away
from the father and daughter.

The windows wear capital-R-shaped curtains,
and the doorknob is colored black,
drawn big enough that a good father,
if he forgot his key, could open
the front door and come home,

but if it's night and he's the bad father,
he won't be able to see the doorknob
until tomorrow when the good father returns.

A gray cat should be colored in, hunting
mice to hide under the kitchen table,
and a red cocker spaniel, old and fussy,
biting company because his ears hurt.

The little girl should be running
across the yard yelling, "Hurry up!"
to her baby brother, not in the picture
because he isn't born for three more years,
but she misses him already.

It should be raining all over this picture,
not just under the single white cloud,
raining on the mother in her red coat
until she looks toward the little girl,

raining on the father's car until
he stops driving and walks back
to stand on the green strip of yard

with the mother and daughter,
so they'll all be smiling big smiles,
way up above their ears,
like they already are in this picture.

Kiss, Kiss

To win the war, my father supplies
the island of New Caledonia
with gin, Scotch, whatever.

He writes, "Keep the home fires
burning," sends colored photographs.

In one, he wears white shorts
as two native girls in flowered tops
and wrap-around skirts cling

to his arms, all three of them smiling.

My mother cuts away the girls
with curved fingernail scissors,
crumples the letter into an ashtray,

touches it off with her silver lighter.
After it's burning nicely, she
throws in the girls, then frames

the picture of her husband,
sets it on the bedroom dresser.

...

An old friend informs my father
by letter that his wife
has gone out with another man.

My mother never denies it, intro-
duces him to me, five years old.

He's just a friend, they don't
even kiss. If she had her way,
she'd have her own bedroom.

A peck on the cheek
and be done with it.

...

My father comes home from the war,
eyes narrowing to slits
under the influence of anger
mixed with dry martinis.

It always begins at night
in the living room. I'm alseep,
slowly wake to angry voices,

rising. One thing thrown, another
tipped over, there's a ritual
to these affairs. I'm awake now.

Every time, the same trial:
(It's begun again without me.)
Who did what to whom.

I must serve as judge and jury.
Throwing back the covers, I put on
my green robe, red flannel slippers,

hurry down the hall toward the living
room, attend the night's proceedings.

...

He doesn't have to use his fists
to send my mother flying.

A body hitting the wall
sounds duller than a full glass.

...

In my bedroom, he's killing her
again, traps her against my bunk beds
covered with cowboy spreads,

his hands around her neck, her face
darkening with her own stopped
blood. On my top bunk, the fuzzy ears
of my stuffed rabbit wiggle.

My Lone Ranger ring glows in the dark
from its blue box on the dresser.

When I run at my father
with a butcher knife held high
above my head, I mean to run

the knife through him, mean to kill
him without heart, the way a grizzly
gone loco is killed.

...

But the heart will not stay
out of it. Come morning,
we're still alive.

...

When the nightmares recur,
I scream the words
they've thrown at one another.

Mother, embarrassed, touches
my shoulder to wake me.
I'm frightened at first, think
they're fighting again, then see

her worried face, vow to try harder
not to upset her.

...

"Kiss good-night," I call out
from my top bunk to their bedroom.
They know I can't sleep until they do.

Mother calls back in a silly
sing-song voice, "I'm walking over
to daddy's bed now, and now,

I'm kissing your daddy." She mimics
the affection, "Kiss, kiss."

Second World War Casualties

During the war, Mother and I
live with my grandfather, sleep
in his back room. When December
arrives and war still rages,

he plays Santa, first teasing me:
"Don't expect any Christmas
this year," he says, "the Japs

have shot the old boy down!"
By the last Christmas of the war,
I know it's him under that
silly beard, pretend I don't.

He's been sick. The red suit
hangs loosely as he hands me

a China doll, her face both woman
and child, cheeks paler than pink.

All winter, I dress and undress her,
as he cheers on the Allied advances.
When his body finally surrenders
to cancer, I sit on his bed

rocking my doll until even that
small movement hurts him.

Waving good-bye as the ambulance
takes him on his last ride,
clumsy in my sorrow,
I stumble, drop the doll

who falls head first, her China face
shattering across the asphalt.

I try to love her anyway, sit on
his empty bed, rock her and sing,
until I stuff the faceless body
in the trash, pink dress and all,

vow never to play with dolls again.
Then I see, through my tears,
a herd of wild horses. They gallop
to me, neigh and toss their heads.

I don't choose the white one
or the one whose coat shines gold
in the sun, I pick the black,

who rears and paws the sky.
I choose the one no one can break.

Mounting, I gallop away from the house
toward the cloudy peaks
I can barely see in the distance.

Fallout

Childhood mornings, black sheet
covering a cold sun, I balanced,
barefoot, on the heated grate
of the floor radiator, dressing in warm
clothes my mother spread across
a wooden chair the night before.
Hurrying my feet through the holes,
her hands shook. Anxious mouth
daubed red, eyelid drooping,
she could see inside my clothes:
something there scared her

and she looked away.
Dangerous wind off the Idaho desert
scratched against our windows
like the snow again today. Dressing
in what I've laid out, Mother is still
here, worried. "Go on," she says,
"perhaps you can do it." Then, she
watches for me to stumble or fall.
Not that she wants me to fall,
exactly, but she's without
a word for not falling.

How To Be Lucky

practice tying bows until
they stay tied & learn
your left & right so you'll
know exactly when to turn,
& saying prayers, bless
everyone, but do not think
of bob, who shot himself,
& stock up on supplies:
paper, pencils, ruler,
& write your thank-yous
keeping every line straight,
& don't forget capitals:
b is for boise, capitol
of Idaho, where bob died,
& never share nightmares,
especially with your parents—
if adults believe a nightmare,
it comes true—& when you
think bad thoughts about
your mother, or say them out
in anger, even if you take
them back & whirl around
three times saying, mercy
on me, when your mother dies
you've made yourself an orphan
& never say the word divorce:
to have luck, *you must get*
perfect

Fool's Gold

When Father gets mad at Mother,
his voice changes, how he says her name
changes. Usually he just talks to her
in his telephone voice, but when she's
burned the meat again or poured bleach
straight out of the bottle to eat holes
in his white dress shirts, his voice
lowers, he calls her "Jo-se-phine,"
the syllables all separate from one
another in a voice hard as cooled
lava, each crease a canyon.

When Father calls Mother "Jo-se-phine"
in that hard voice of his, Mother's face
changes. Her eyes—black lashes curled,
thickened with mascara—grow wider, innocent
as a lamb. Her voice rises, gets smaller.
"What is it, Dear?" she says, the "Dear" trailing
off like a pebble dropped into a canyon,
but she's not waiting around until it lands,
she's busy wiping off the kitchen table
scrubbed just moments ago, busy
being good as gold.

Accidental Deaths

Beside the driveway, a huge evergreen
shades the dog my mother has loved
since she was little. Old and deaf,

the red cocker spaniel stretches out
under the tree to cool off. We come back
from a family outing—my father drives.

When we turn into the driveway, the sun's
in his eyes, he can't see. The car jumps

a little as the wheels go over the dog,
who's always been a grouchy dog, snapping
at people, especially my father, but now

he flops around like he's trying to be funny.
Mother jumps out of the car, screaming,
kneels beside the bouncing dog,

hands above her head, fingers
stretched up to a clear sky.

My father stands awkwardly above her
and the dog, saying, "He's dead, Josephine,"
meaning, the dog feels no pain, but this

only makes her scream louder. She looks up
at him and we all know she thinks

he did it on purpose. She jerks away when
he tries to touch her shoulder.

"He's dead," my father repeats, "come inside now,"
and guides her, sobbing, toward the house,
leaving me alone in the car, engine running,

alone with the dog, legs moving him
toward what's already gone.

One More For The Road

1.

Southern Idaho is bare except for
sagebrush, tumbleweeds, and steaming
lava cooled into heaps of stone.

The sameness of the straight highway
is broken by jackrabbits
dead on the road
like flies on sticky paper.

The little girl counts them
to sleep, stopping when
her head nods
somewhere in the hundreds.

Rising out of the desert, each town
is an oasis offering one hotel,
several bars, and, maybe,
one movie theatre.

Shoshone, Picabo, Aberdeen, Bliss:
towns forged from promises.

She sits on stools drinking Coke
in bars smelling of greased sawdust.
Old men ask her questions

that don't need answers,
jiggle her on their knees
smiling their brown-teeth smiles.

Her father's driving speed spirals
with each stop until, by dark,

their car claims the whole highway,
axles trembling with the strain.

During the day, she stands on the seat
between her parents, head almost touching
the material, soft and gray, across the roof,
or she pulls hard to lower the armrest
and sit on it, looking straight ahead.

She reads the familiar Burma Shave ads
lining the highway or laughs and sings
old Navy songs with her father
over her mother's ignored frown.

They shout out all the verses
of Cocaine Bill and Morphine Sue:
"Honey have a (sniff), have a (sniff)
on me! Honey have a (sniff) on me!
Honey have a (sniff), have a (sniff)
on me! Honey have a (sniff) on me."

But after dark there is only one
solution to fear. On the ledge
behind the back seat,
she curls up small.

The rabbits aren't so bad
if they're behind the car.

She watches the stars, dreams
of a world with no liquor
or loud voices, a world where
jackrabbits look both ways.

2.

Too big to stand on the front seat,
she sits between her parents
or sleeps across the back seat.

She complains about stopping
at every small-town bar,
but they remember prohibition.

Drinking is their protest against
big government running your life
and they never miss a town.

Leaving the smell of liquor
and wood shavings, she goes
exploring, finds footraces,
part of some local celebration.

In spite of hostile stares,
she takes off her cowboy boots
and runs stocking-footed,
fast as a jackrabbit,

wins five races, $25.00, then runs,
victorious, back to the bar.

Out of money, words thickening,
they try to bargain a loan
for just one more drink,

but she rolls up her money tight
as her lips saying no, refuses
the loan at any interest rate.

That night, by dark, they've sobered.
She's too big for the ledge now.
She can't see the stars as well,

but she has $25.00 in her pocket
and sleep without fear
or loud voices.

Sanctuary

For Chad

When the house fills with furious whispers
although it's nearly dark, she must take
her little brother and go. Alone in the forest,

they trip on roots at first but soon
step easily over. She pulls green shoots
to feed him, mimics that plaintive voice
calling them home for supper.

Hand in hand, hand in hand, they spin,
fall back in the damp grass. She paints
red circles on the birch with crushed berries,
smears her forehead blue, as he takes off
his cotton suit, hums into a leaf, and dances.

What does the owl's round eye see
through the night? When ferns curl up,
what do they whisper? Soon, the children sleep,
his head in her lap. He's the good husband,
small and boney, and she's the rosy wife,
the lucky one, until the voices wake them.

Knees and elbows muddy, hair matted
with leaves, the children are carried
toward the fire. "You're safe,"
the parents keep saying. "Safe now."

Bottled

When Mother's drinking, the door to my room
slams shut, sealed with bottle labels.
Brown walls of glass, cracked mirror of moans,
blue curtains drawn, sewn closed with sobs.
No way out. Or in.

How 'bout a drink?

At five, sharp, let the masquerade begin.
What cunning disguises: Wear egg nog for
pleasing Santa, martini for praising the Lord.
Come, raise your voices. Dry! Dry!
Happy Beerday to you....

Can I freshen that up?

Our party's out cold, poor thing, its face
as pale as vodka. Every glass
is broken, every lamp lit.
Grenadine, you sad son-of-a-bitch!
Cocktail onion! Lemon twist! Stuffed olive!

Can I pour you another?

Sit down, won't you? Over there,
on that drunk—he's the sofa. Or that one—
he's a chair. Just give him a drink
before you sit. Then he'll be soft,
won't cause you any trouble.

Just one more?

But when he throws his fist, the light
goes out. My room fills up with a jigger-
and-a-half, the furniture floats and bobbles.
Swallowed by this dark swirl, I swim
toward the blinking neon sign.

Have a little nightcap?

All the drunks are drowned. I can't find
a place to sleep. Ice cubes listen
to my psalms, chilled, and swallowed
straight. Tuck me in, tuck me in.
I love you. You!

Love Letter From Acalpulco

On Mother's dresser,
on the white lace doily,
crocheted by her mother
to catch and hold a younger
marriage, the letter

meant for my father,
the formal Charles,
husband of my mother, who
stares at its thin envelope.

My father's other woman
has entered the house,
the perfume of her letter mixing
with the smell of chicken
Father is cooking
in the kitchen.

Do not speak to Mother now,
who met my father once in secret
at his brother's house.
She called him, "Sugar."

"Mother," he calls her now,
this man, Charles,
who barbecues chicken
in the sauce he stirs
all afternoon.

Do not disturb them,
the gray woman,
the small gray daughter,
as they sit at the edge
of the single bed.

How The Accordion Wars Ended

When Mother, using bribes
or threats, finally got me to play,

my left hand thundered across
the bases for "Night Riders in the Sky."

Dinner parties trembled, paused between
pickled herring and chicken hotdish,
until the Seventh Grade Assembly where,

after a stunning rendition of "Beer
Barrel Polka," cheered back for an encore,

I forgot "Tea for Two" completely,
having focused on getting through one alive.

Seconds passed, too long and silent to reckon.
Then, I bowed, walked off the stage.

When the auditorium finally darkened,
I found Mother waiting grimly in the lobby.
She thought I'd done it on purpose.

We didn't speak. I laid the accordion
in its padded case, black coffin
I never opened again, and never again

did Mother burst into my room during practice,
accuse me of kicking over my music stand,

the bent silver stand I had just caught
and righted with my foot.

Christmas Eve, The Morning After

When Father assembled the Christmas trike
from Santa to my little brother,
he screwed the straight bar into the curved,

but he never got the wheels.
He swore in angry gusts, chanted directions
to himself, then swore again,

but the spell didn't take.
Red-faced, he shouted at Mother
to buy things already assembled,

said if she was so smart, she could
damn well put it together herself,
stalked off to bed. We heard him
muttering directions from the bedroom.

When Father set up the Christmas train,
he got the track together, shiny figure-eight,
crossing over itself, always coming back
to where it started. Blowing till she was giddy,

Mother filled the plastic clown with feet of sand;
I raised the cardboard circus tent,
hung acrobats from their wooden ladders.

Father stared at the picture of wires,
covert connections to infuse the train
with movement and whistle and smoke. He crumpled

up the page, shouted that the train was too
expensive anyway, stalked off to bed.
While brushing his teeth, he slammed the door
of the medicine cabinet three times.

Mother and I knelt as if in prayer,
whispering the foreign words to one another:
switcher, transformer, rerailer—

we stayed up all night giving the train
its warning whistle and smoky puffs.

Christmas morning, Father hummed as he fried
the spiced sausage, made his famous gravy;
he sang "Hallelujah" while he cut
the buttermilk biscuits with a glass
dipped in flour. Mother and I looked

at one another, then at the little boy
riding his red trike across the rug
as his train tooted around its figure-eight.

We were ready to eat when breakfast
was finally served—sausage and gravy,
biscuits, light brown on top, with warm syrup.
Heaping our plates, we accepted any gift given.

Cashmere Disciple

I said nothing but no,
did nothing but yes,
teen-aged, dressing up,
imitating those adults
whose lives I didn't want

to wear. My first job
was selling sweaters to rich
Southern Californians who
unfolded their money
like daily prayers.

I, too, believed, spent every-
thing I earned, bought
32 expensive cashmere
sweaters, wearing them
with matching skirts
and matching socks, rolled
down below the ankle bones
above the white buck shoes.

Each rainbow sweater cost
more than my family's food
for a week, 32 prayers
that couldn't save me—
I knew it even then—
and bought anyhow.

Helen Hart's Summer Watercolor Class

She wore gold earrings
big as Kerr Jar lids,
and a purple scarf waving behind

her yellow jeep for blocks
as she picked us up for watercolor class.
She drove faster than our mother's
voices calling us home.

Instead of aprons, she wore eyelashes
so long and black we couldn't
take our eyes off them. Her work
was our play, her play, our delight,

and her laugh sailed every pond
in Julie Davis Park, startling
the iridescent mallards
we girls painted, greens flowing
into blues, blues into greens.

Round-eyed, we stared up at gigantic
trees reaching over the still pond,
tried to take them in, couldn't keep them

on the page, leaves greening off
into blue's washed sky, trunks
dripping brown onto our bare toes.

It was the summer we wanted
to last beyond the white pages
of our artist pads,

until the next year when we discovered
boys and, blooming inside us, the roses
we'd only red-dotted on the page,

and lost our vision, stored our brushes
in metal tins, trees shrunk down to salt
and sugar, measured, then spooned
into nested silver bowls. We baked white
bread and brownies, timed everything,

nearly forgot where we'd hidden our colors—
the murmur of blue, red's rejoicing,
violet's tenor enhancing yellow's aria—

frozen squares of color, waiting for
the brush, a drop of water, background
light enough to let us through.

II.

Reaching Out In The Dark

Swimming After The Turtle

1.

Day after pitiless day,
the woman spins her kidneys
into cocktail cherries.
Even at the end, she bleeds
visibly, an embarrassing display.
But she learns death well,
passes on everything she knows
to her daughter, who wears
her own frail flesh and blood
like a party dress. Flying over
a chromium ocean, the daughter
scatters her mother's ashes,
cannot look down.

2.

In the city, an older woman
lives alone. Having cocktails
on her little balcony, she wears white.
New white building, white pearls
softening her sixty years.
"Two months," the doctor said. Tonight,
she doubles what she pours her soda into,
then she will plan her own funeral.
From her balcony on eighth floor,
she studies the landscape
of the parking lot, the small
bouquets of stones.

3.

Another woman lives in a crumbling
building without balconies.
The week they tear it down
for renewal, he beats her again,
breaks her face. Winter,
windows iced inside, only salt
left in the kitchen cupboard.
The children crying
is what gets to him.

4.

Taking off her black dress,
a woman dives head-first
into deep water,
swims after the turtle.
Its shell cut in two, the front
half, neck stretched forward,
paddles like it will never stop.
Bits of turtle flesh trail
from the shell like ribbons.
The woman swims eagerly,
as if she really believes
she will catch and hold it.
How smooth her body,
glowing white, how gigantic
her human desire!

In The Hands Of The Lake

On November 10, 1975, the
Edmund Fitzgerald went down
during a violent storm on Lake
Superior. All 29 crew members
were trapped inside the ship.

1.

The first cold day.
A solitary duck,
swimming in windy circles,
seems the bravest
thing alive.

2.

Starting tonight,
my love and I
will only speak
of winter scientifically.
Our lab is under cover
of a thick green blanket,
our Bunsen burners
turned up high,
notebooks hidden
under our pillows.

3.

Beneath the orange lifeboats
on Lake Superior,
the sailors are trapped
in the cracked hull
of the ship—

they swim, head first,
arms back, like babies,
cupped in the hands
of the lake.

4.

On second thought,
tonight we must undress,
lie on top of the blanket.
I will touch the fur
on your chest with
a flat palm, feel it
resist me. Cold
and hot, hot and cold,
your naked body—

5.

We will live
as if winter
were only a tiny
rhinestone hidden
in your palm,
or a sunflower shell
carried under my tongue.

Cooking Catalogue

On a cool September day, the soup commences:
vegetable beef, its vitamins an orange and green
rainbow, its sky dotted with beef, the dark
storms of carnivores. Then split peas, solidly
green or yellow all the way through. I soak them,
boil them until they give their sandy gift,
wrapped in ham smoke and salt. And turkey noodle:
breaking the empty carcass, boiling it,
dark meat and white relaxing from the dancing bones.
My kitchen a smorgasbord of smells, I ladle
steaming soup into seven bowls. At the table,
six people take and eat, while I lean back, full,
and watch an early snow stir and blow outside.

When lilacs unlock their buds, it's salad time:
tuna salad, celery a crisp parenthesis
around slipshod macaroni. Radishes snapping
back at the bite; thin cucumber wheels and purple
onions roll me away in shivers; boiled eggs
gussied up with mustard and green chives. And artichoke,
the queen of vegetables, the sharp-tongued ruler.
Green crown shined and oiled, her layered
wisdom begins with justice only but ends with mercy
and butter melted and lemon mayonnaise.
Oh the feast of it all! Oh spring!
Pass the salad, pass the iced tea,
pass the lilacs for a second smell.

Weekend In The Country

> Hope, the dream
> of those who wake.

Away from the city, our pleasure
moves us slowly. Curled all day
under a patchwork quilt with a book
of Paula Becker's paintings, I disrupt

the graceful flow of your Tai Chi, show
you the ones I love. Her self-portrait,
naked to the waist, wearing aqua beads,
fruit and flowers revealed in her skin.

I read aloud what she has written
about her painting of old Bredow,
who philosophised, walking his friend,
the cow, lightly tapping her flank
every step with a stick.

Together we study his sad face, gouged
by the excavations of drink and bad
living, who has finally, Becker writes,
found evening peace in the poorhouse.

Watching your arms and legs move in unison,
I can see your faith in abundance,
in order through change, as sunset,
behind you in the window, outlines
in flame your motive grace. I savor
your body's familiar landscape: such
happiness, too much happiness
to contain, then, suddenly, fear.

Behind your slow dance, snow on the hills
burns red, then fades. All around us,
so many dark houses, faces individually
shaded, even those living in pairs.

Paula Becker, before dying in child-
birth, painted old Bredow, who, in spite of
his badgering brother, the aristocrat
of their birth, chose his quiet dreaming
and the cow. Closing the book I wanted
never to end, I stand to embrace you,

turn toward the window, open my arms
to the world, then, shivering, climb back
in my warm bed. The sun drops,
the pines blacken. You look at me,
so much love in your look,
seeing something I can't.

Menses

This unclenched human fist
measures the blind ache of fish
curving seaward, the slip
of lava into softer
configurations. No language
can encompass this longing.
Come to me now, gather up
my languid arms and legs,
rock me like the child
we haven't begun. Listing back
and forth, a single empty boat,
we'll drift to the tenebrious
hum of endings without end.

Melancholy

1.

Because he's unhappy, she knows it must be her fault.
The woman figures heavily in these things.
Or is it his mother? Or that she reminds him
of his mother? The way she holds her coffee cup.
The color green.

2.

These days she's wearing browns and blues.
Nothing helps. His hands grow cold as galoshes.
One night she wakes and watches him. His mouth
is moving: open and shut, open and shut.
His hands paddle silently at his sides.

She still loves him. Forever and always,
and again, always. She begins holding her coffee cup
in her left hand. Stops drinking coffee altogether.
His eyes grow bigger, rounder. They never close.

3.

He takes no suitcase. Walks out the front door
wearing his corduroy jacket. It fits strangely
over his back fin. She doesn't try to stop him.
Later, a postcard from Key West saying
the weather's mild, the water's warm.

4.

She's doing fine, really, the one who was two
who has now become one. Or is it the two who
were one who have now become two? She's confused.
Nothing is simple anymore. But not drinking coffee
is better for her nerves and she's grown fond
of browns and blues. When people ask, she says
he's traveling—on business.

5.

It gets lonely. She talks to his picture.
Sings to herself. Snacks on nuts and berries.
Lately, she's had the urge to fly, to find him.
She feels he needs her. This morning, showering,
she finds one white feather growing under her arm.

Attitudes Of Thanksgiving

Last winter, everything iced over:
houses, streets, desire, even mild
affection. Our talk trailed off

into snow flurries, our Monet painting
of water lilies froze white on white.
You and I curled up in our cold
separate lives, drifted into deep
slumber, occasionally reaching out
in the dark, but seldom touching.
In this climate, winter kills.

It also ends, and, like the last survivor,
I take nothing for granted. April,
the world is about to be born again,
and this time I'll be there to see it.
Impatient for green leaves, the hallelujahs
of tulips, I walk to the lake

without a coat. Shivering, I feel the sun
on my face. Bathsheba, our black lab,
looking neither up nor down, trots
through broken bottles of Miller's and Hamm's,
danger with no warning smell. Canada geese
stand awkwardly courting on the spongy ice.

You look at me like I'm that garden
greening behind the thorned hedge—
I accept your radiant gifts and again
dream in color. Later, waking, we recall
dark winter mornings, as our bodies
melt into attitudes of thanksgiving.

Blue Heron, Wind, The River

1.

As wind turns the river
against us, we paddle
our sluggish canoe.

Around every bend
another blue heron
rises

from silence to silence, wings
trailing the silver body behind.

We cannot know
whether the next heron
is the same one
flown ahead,

or another, fellow
acolytes of sky
and flight. Either way,
a miracle,

though the river makes no
distinction, and the sun
extends the same gift

of shadow to a tree log
or a human body, floating
face down, limbs trailing off
into fingered leaves.

2.

When the clear sky blackens
and the wind declares war,
we tie our canoe, wind-break,
between trees, then pitch
our tent behind it.

All night, tornado winds
try to shake us
from our small tent,
trees lurch above us
like drunken giants.

We sing to one another,
our voices slender threads
inside this cage of wind.

There's nothing to be done
but wait, so you begin the song
our bodies know, leading,
while I follow, then I
go on ahead and you
catch up, creating

our private storm,
its own abate, and calm
sleep in one feathered bag,

lightning striking
all night, our dreams
blazing unnatural with light.

When dawn reddens
our tent, it is quiet.

We touch each other
in mute wonder, touch
our own faces, huge trees
down all around us.

3.

Between the gawking flap
of wing against wave
and the glide of smooth flight,
that moment of ascent,

that moment we paddle for
with all our unfeathered lives,

though the wind blows harder
than we can push and we forget
which way the river
is flowing. We open our lives

to whatever wind, imitate
even that we cannot name,
rising, always rising,
at the far edge of our eye.

III.

Unlocking The Doors

Unlocking The Doors

1.

One night, I saw a woman
jerk away from a man, run
for her life, but he ran faster.

"Get help!" I called to my friend,
ran after the woman. When she tripped,
he was on her, a big man, kicking
her ribs, her face,

then standing her up, walking her.
I caught up to them, took her arm,
asked, "Do you need help?"

"Willie," she pleaded, I looked at him,
repeated his name, "Willie,
she doesn't want to go,"

his fist clenched her collar.
I would not let go of her arm.

My friend brought two policemen,
I pulled the woman away. Crying
now, her head ached, her name
was Debbie from San Diego,
since fourteen she'd been on her own.

I kept my arm around her in the car.
They had one bed left at the shelter,
they took her in.

2.

A man who beats his woman
arms himself with small excuses.

They have one plate, one
fork between them, share,
until the woman, careless,

drops the fork. She croons his name,
brushes his hair, sits quietly
next to him, but she can never

sit still enough; when he accuses,
she denies, his eyes dilate,
go steel, he raises his fist.

Who will hear her scream? She's alone
with a killer who will kill her slowly—

Later, he touches where the woman hurts,
marvels at her small wrists, the way
her hips hide jungles inside them.
He is always worse than he meant.

3.

My own mother, her two black eyes,
her swollen upper lip,

how I wanted her arm around me
when we slept all night in the car,
coming in at dawn before the neighbors saw,
when we huddled in the bedroom,

him beating against the door,
the door bending toward us, groaning.

Night after dark night, I must
save her, even when she hits
first. How the small ones despise
weakness, he was what I loved,

what we both loved,
so when we hid in the bathroom
and she pressed her back against
his weight on the other side,

screaming, "No! No!"
to his, "Let me in!"

and when she made a bed
for me in the bathtub
out of soft pink towels,

even then I could not thank her,
she could not look me in the eye.

If now, in the light of morning,
she could finally unlock the door,
if only I could take her
by the arm and not let go.

Transmutations

Cancer is shrinking my tall father.
Our voices hush as he grows smaller,
I grow younger: a college girl
again, showing him my dorm—
the plaid curtains, the matching spread.

Running back home from grade school,
white dots bouncing on my navy dress,
I bring him straight A's.

In my playpen, I babble,
"Daddy's girl," while he leans
on his black cane in my huge baby hand,

the hand that cannot hold him
in his skin and bones. Dropping back
to embryo, I'll sail that glassy stream
toward the luminous union,

while my father, in a distant sky,
soars upward by the thousands.

My Mother's Hands

Puffy as blown-up rubber gloves,
each stubby finger groped
for some happiness she never
grasped. Those hands forecast
her disposition by the violence
of their shaking. When she'd
been drinking, they flopped
around her lap like wet birds.
After her death, the jeweler near
her office said she came in
every day during lunch hour
and tried on rings, stretching out
her fingers to look at the glimmer
of rubies and emeralds she never
owned, gems to refresh hands
tired from typing insurance forms
turned in by the rich claiming
money for their stolen goods,
hands I give this poem to,
bloated swans, chapped lily-red.

Hunger

My heart
is an open

mouth. My mouth
is an open

grave. Even
my life

cannot fill it.

Salesman Of The Year

My father, the towheaded boy, who daily trailed after
the cart of the Chinese vegetable vender, was lucky
in looks, but, in the white stare of the desert, he'd
heard the coyote's lean warning & listened & escaped
the herding of sheep by taking shortcuts, worshipping
Uncle Grover, who castrated lambs, knife held between
his teeth, & Grover informed him that money was freedom
& easy & so he borrowed & traded & stole
& dealt cars—Kaiser-Fraser, Lincoln, or Cadillac—
selling every car with all accessories included,
& then, the big deal, the one that would do it,
exporting Chinese to Caracas, which sent him to prison,
but soon back to cars, earning three closets full
of cashmere sport coats, twenty pairs of shoes, handmade
in Hong Kong, silk shirts initialed C.C.B., seventeen
disposable razors because he never liked to run out,
every western novel ever written by Louis L'Amour,
& when he weakened from the cancer that took him
off the Lincoln car lot—Salesman of the Year—he read
mail order catalogues, ordered gold carpeting
for the house, new mattresses, teflon frypans, & clocks
that cuckooed or chimed or both & the bills came
after he died, with nothing but words in the will,
&, near the end, he saw diamondback rattlers
curled sunning on the asphalt of his hospital bed,
& never a man not to complain, he ranted at Mother,
at the nurses, raved at the doctor, the white walls,
except for when he was praying, a late career,
& on his nightstand, next to Oral Roberts' book,
next to a letter from The Ladies of Lourdes, Iowa,
who reassured him over five thousand Capuchin monks
were praying for him twice daily for the ten dollars

his wife so kindly contributed, was the sign:
"I Believe In Miracles," & he took his last communion
scolding Mother and me because we whispered once
& he wanted it religious, but no fancy dancy church affair
& as my father's favorite & only daughter,
at the end, when he, already in the cloudy sky of death,
pointed at the blank wall, to the cuckoo clock he'd ordered,
not hanging there since it hadn't yet arrived,
& when he asked me what time it was,
I said it was still early.
Two days later, among the patio plants he had carefully
watered, on the concrete he hosed down daily,
we had a small service, lighting a candle
on the T.V. tray where he'd eaten for twenty years, mean
on or off martinis, haranguing his favorite six o'clock
newsman, & Mother read The Twenty-Third Psalm,
& my brother, an Episcopal prayer for the dead,
that church he joined to meet the people he needed
to know when he made it & I read two poems about him
and a letter from the boys at the Lincoln car lot
saying no one could sell a car like Charlie,
& we all went out & ate a big meal
at the Chinese restaurant he loved, & Benny, the owner,
wept for him, said he was the finest man he'd ever met
& brought out his favorite, pork & sesame, on the house,
& I returned to my own life, this latest act of faith,
all accessories included.

The Benediction Of Horses

I walk naked through the crowded barn,
horses standing rump to flank,
their breath steaming.

I must edge between them,
arms at my sides, polite as a child
caught in a large party of adults,

a child whose parents are
somewhere in the smoky room,
their glasses between them,

speaking toward one another through
the sharp medium of gin, voices
slurred now, first in laughter,
then, with accusation's twisted lips.

At the far side of the barn I discover
the oldest horse, an ancient woman,
who sleeps all day on a bench,
her head-scarf black as the stallion
guarding this sanctuary from nightmare.

Under the bench sleeps her child, a pinto
colt. I pick it up, hold it like a baby,
as it reaches toward me with soft cat paws.

When I place it on the dirt floor, it grows
large as an Indian pony and I ride it bareback
through the barn that smells of urine
and damp earth, the horses, their massive
heated bodies, stepping aside, protective.

All night we ride the streets of the city,
deserted under the merciful eye of the moon.
We are so still, rider and horse, on soft
cat feet, disturbing nothing.

When we ride back to the party, the glasses
are washed and put away, the couples sit
quietly, little children holding hands.

My horse, again a colt, chooses my child mother
to curl up beside, and, in the clear shape
of a breeze, I fly between my little mother's legs,
up inside her to the purple comfort of her flesh,
waiting for this loneliness called life.